HEREAFTER

Hereafter

Is there life beyond death?

by

DAVID WINTER

MOWBRAY
LONDON & OXFORD

Contents

Preface

In the eight years since this book was first published a great deal has happened to increase interest in its subject. If the sixties was the decade of outer space, with probes and manned space-ships pushing back the boundaries of our knowledge about the universe, the seventies was the decade of inner space. We had looked out, and become aware of our smallness in the echoing emptiness of the universe. So now we looked in, to discover, or re-discover, what manner of thing we are, to be sure that we really do exist and have meaning and value. The seventies was the decade of meditation and contemplation, when 'spiritual' began to take over from 'scientific' as the word to use if you wanted to indicate that an idea or proposal was valuable and authentic.

Part of that search for inner reality was concerned with mankind's ultimate destiny, and especially with life beyond death. It was fascinating to watch how interest in this subject grew during the seventies. Books covered every aspect, from a scholarly treatment of the idea of eternal life in all the world's religions (*Death and Eternal Life*, Ed. J. Hick, SCM), to several compilations of the testimonies of people who had 'died' for short periods of time and had experienced visions or revelations of life 'on the other side' (e.g. *Life after Death*, Kingsway).

However, there was still a marked reluctance to take seriously the traditional Christian belief in resurrection. It seemed that any strange notion was to be entertained, no matter how exotic, grotesque or unlikely, except the belief that has done more to shape for the better our own civilisation than anything else.

Indeed, when it is taken seriously it still has the same effect. I have been delighted, and moved, by the hundreds of letters I have received in response to *Hereafter*, from people of all ages and from every part of our society. Some have expressed their gratitude for a book which puts into words beliefs which they have felt rather than fully grasped. Some have said what a relief it was to find that the most attractive of all doctrines of survival, the Christian one, is also so consistent, convincing and reasonable.

But the most moving letters have come from older people and from those who have been bereaved. One woman in particular, who described herself as having a more than academic interest in the subject, 'being in her eighties', wrote to say that through reading the book she was now, for the first time in her life, able to believe that life does not end at death, and that new-found faith had brought her great joy and comfort.

For some, the comfort has been even more dramatic. One woman wrote to tell me how she was going through the personal papers of her mother, who had died a few days before. Suddenly she was overcome with grief and with doubt about the whole idea of the resurrection of the dead (although she and her mother were Roman Catholics). She began to cry, and the tears fell on the papers in front of her. She picked up the papers to move them, and found that on the top of the pile was a copy of *Hereafter*, which her mother had obviously been reading. It was, as she said, like a personal message of comfort.

DAVID WINTER

Introduction

'There is darkness without, and when I die there will be darkness within. There is no splendour, no vastness anywhere; only triviality for a moment, and then nothing.' So wrote Bertrand Russell before his death, and in two sentences he captured what many, many people today feel about life and death.

In the 60's man reached out into space. In the 70's he probed inward to the mysteries of the human mind and body. In both processes he fell victim to his own cleverness. In trying to become god, he convinced himself he was a machine. In trying to defeat death, he gave it its greatest victory. Perhaps for the first time in human history we have a whole civilisation that lives as though there is nothing beyond death: darkness ... and nothing.

Certainly people today lack any convincing faith to the contrary. Every survey of public opinion in Britain since the Second World War has shown a decrease in the number of those who believe in life beyond death. Some of this, of course, merely reflects a general cynicism about religious commitment of every kind. But even 'religious' people, churchgoers of all denominations, are among those who express doubt about the doctrine of the resurrection. Indeed, it is a matter of simple observation that even those who profess their belief in the doctrine do not live as though death were a door opening on a new and better life. Rather, it is quite obviously regarded as an unwelcome intruder, to be ignored for as long as we can, and then disposed of as quickly and inconspicuously as possible. Few sermons are preached on the subject, and when Christians set out to win unbelievers, the prospect of heaven is held up as an incentive to faith about as often as the prospect of hell is.

Most of those who now reject the idea of 'survival' after death have been consciously or subconsciously influenced by the materialism of this century, and by materialistic science. They believe – often simply on hearsay or general impression – that 'science' (whatever that is) has 'disproved' (whatever that means) any idea of 'immortality'. They may have heard the vivid phrase of philosopher Gilbert Ryle, 'There is no ghost in the human machine.' Certainly the spectacular advance of space science and of knowledge about the universe has undermined the faith of those who believed in a crudely literal 'heaven' 'above the bright blue sky'. We all know that 'above the bright blue sky' is a lot more sky, and then a lot more: millions of light years of it.

Equally the advance of knowledge about ourselves – the processes of our minds, our origins, our bodies – has diluted the sense of wonder and mystery about mankind, the peak of creation. Whether our scientific curiosity has taken us out to space or into the human psyche, we have found no pearly gates, no immortal soul.

Obviously many of the old ideas are wrong, at the factual scientific level. But with those superstitious and pseudo-biblical notions has gone the whole concept of a life beyond this life, entered into through what we call death.

The object of this book is to help to bring it back again; to show that, properly understood, there is nothing impossible or even unlikely about 'life after death'. Indeed, that many modern discoveries and insights make it easier to accept now than it could ever have been for a Victorian. In the process of exploring this subject I shall hope to show that to reject the very idea of life after death is unreasonable prejudice, requiring as firmly closed a mind as it is often alleged is needed to believe in it.

Life beyond death is, I believe, an essential part of the good news that God revealed in Jesus Christ. It is a part of the Christian faith that modern man needs as much as, or more than, any other; a belief that transforms our whole attitude to life, as well as to death. I believe that ordinary people have totally misunderstood what 'science' does, and does not, say in this area, and have had a priceless element of the good life stolen from them without realising it.

'There is no death, but the people do not believe it.' So J. Paterson Smyth wrote in his classic tract *The Gospel of the Hereafter* seventy years ago.[1] There is no 'darkness', no empty void, beyond. There is no end to the progress of human personality, because there is no end to God, who is its fixed point. There is no need to fear. That is the Christian position, and it is one that can bear any examination. I do not say that anyone can prove that there is life after death but I would claim that anyone who comes without prejudice to the evidence will at least have to agree with the famous brain specialist, Sir John Eccles, who said, 'I cannot believe that the gift of conscious experience has no further future, no possibility of another existence under some other intangible conditions. At least I would maintain that this possibility of a future existence cannot be denied on scientific grounds.[2]

This book is simply a provocative attempt to make twentieth-century people look again at something that has meant so much to past generations, and has been needlessly and arbitrarily rejected by the very age that needs it most.

NOTES

[1] Hodder.
[2] Quoted in the symposium *Man's Concern with Death*, Hodder, 1968.

Chapter One

MODERN MAN LOOKS AT DEATH

The little girl splashed through a puddle and got mud on her socks. After examining it with a critical eye she asked her mother, 'What's mud for?'

Mother searched rapidly for a convincing answer, and found it. 'For making bricks, dear.'

'What are bricks for?'

'Making houses, dear.'

'What are houses for?'

'People.'

The little girl only paused for a second, and then asked the question to which her mother had no reply.

'And what are people for?'

It is the question modern man hides from, and yet without it, all his other questions and all his elaborate answers to them are so much whistling in the dark.

Previous generations, which had no idea at all how magnetism worked, or how radio waves operated, had satisfying and consistent answers to the question of the nature and destiny of man. Part of our modern dilemma is that we have found out how but we have forgotten why.

Man's life, in terms of cosmic time, is the mere spitting of a tiny spark in the darkness, so brief that it can hardly be seen. And yet these brief human lives have achieved so much, in terms of art and beauty, of creativity and science. It is hard to accept that man's destiny is to turn to dust on the surface of this tiny planet. Indeed, until the present day, the great majority of people have believed that his destiny lay far beyond it, in some future life beyond physical death.

But we have lost that belief, regarding it as too naïve, too unscientific for our more sophisticated age. And with it we have lost a whole dimension of life. Man has reached out to the stars, but shackled his feet to time and space.

It seems a long way from the days when the ambition of many a Christian was to 'make a good death', to his modern counterpart who spends his life trying to postpone it and hoping that he will meet it suddenly and unawares. We speak with envy of the man or woman instantly taken away by a sudden heart attack: he 'knew nothing about it', it was 'mercifully swift'. All sorts of conspiracies are indulged in to keep from the dying person a knowledge of his true condition, and when he finally dies enormous precautions are taken to ensure that his passing upsets or disturbs as few people as possible. An elaborate and extensive industry has grown up to deal with the mechanics of death and burial – or rather, the cosmetics of it, disguising its reality behind elaborate floral arrangements, carefully chosen euphemisms and soothing recorded religious music. The dead – who were a source of inspiration and comfort to our forefathers –

are frankly an embarrassment to us. They remind us of our own mortality, and we prefer to think ourselves immortal.

It is a strange fact that many an adult Western European has never actually seen anybody die. When we consider that over fourteen thousand people die in Britain every week, we see how effectively we have curtained ourselves off from reality. Death happens to everyone, once in every seventy years or so. We are all aware of this, but by some trick of self-deception what we are really thinking is that death happens to everyone else.

In an age when almost everybody believed that 'it is appointed for men to die once, and after that comes judgement',[1] this belief moulded a man's life. He lived with one eye on eternity. This was by no means a morbid obsession. Far from being terrified of death, he prepared for it all his days and faced it not only as the completion of a life well lived but as the transition to a new life. Modern man, with his arid materialism, is more worried by death, more anxious about what he sees as his extinction when it happens, and less confident of his ability to cope with it either in prospect or in the event.

This, it is generally agreed, has become the age of neurosis – and much of this neurosis undoubtedly flows from an inability to come to terms with death. Without any real hope of life beyond it, many people have settled for a philosophy of the absurd. Life has become, for them, a 'tale told by an idiot, full of sound and fury, signifying nothing'. If life is absurd – a meaningless chemical accident, without purpose or destiny – then there is no point in seeking for meaning or reality. We might as well throw in our hands now.

Most people, one imagines, are not so much unbelievers in life beyond as sceptics. It is always dangerous to speculate, but from many conversations with people on this topic I am sure that most would have said that the whole idea of heaven and the 'life hereafter' is just wishful thinking, sharply contradicted by modern science and knowledge; and that beyond arriving at that conclusion very few people would have given the matter much thought.

In other words, the question of life after death is not so much settled as ignored. To face it and think it through would involve raising too many disturbing questions, so it is simply not faced.

But it will not do to leave it like that. To ignore this question is the attitude of the moral coward. It is important: surely everyone would agree. Whether death destroys personality, or is a step onwards to a new life in a new environment, is a momentous question, which every person ought to face, consider, and in due course answer. It is possible to come to terms with death from a thoroughly mature, considered humanistic position; and it is manifestly possible to do so from a mature, considered Christian position. But it is difficult, if not impossible, to do so if our attitude is to refuse to consider the question at all. That way we condemn ourselves to a life-time of self-deception and corroding inner fear, unable to accept either mortality or immortality, either a noble humanism that faces death as the final extinction of a life well lived, or a true Christianity which looks on and beyond to a life with God.

It is essential, then, to face the question of death. Very many of the psychological ills of modern man arise from a failure or refusal to do so. Those who are tempted to dismiss a book on this subject must ask themselves why they are motivated to do so. If the question of life after death is important – and how can it be considered as less? – then a refusal to face it and think it through can only arise from a deep and probably irrational fear.

Mind you, not all who set out to answer the question arrive at either the fully humanist or the fully Christian answers. Some of the other answers we shall be examining later – spiritualism, reincarnation, and other religious beliefs about life after death – but they do not affect very greatly the most basic question of all: does a person cease to be at death, or is there any sense in which personality can survive the physical experience which we call death? To that one can answer yes, no, or not proven. What I find unacceptable is to answer that I prefer not to consider the subject at all. And yet that, I fear, has been the majority verdict in Britain for many years.

Strangely, at the same time interest and participation in the whole area of the mystical and the occult has increased. Possibly because the churches – for the most part – have kept silence on the whole subject, some people have turned to spiritualism, clairvoyance, mysticism, and the occult for answers to their questions and anxieties about death. There is no doubt at all that there has been an enormous increase of interest in what we could broadly call the 'supernatural'. Outbreaks of occult practices and even black magic are frequently reported in the newspapers.

But dabbling in the occult is no real substitute for facing the basic questions about death. Those who have seriously and thoughtfully faced those questions are undoubtedly outnumbered by those who have chosen not to care. To quote Paterson Smyth again: 'Men pass into the Unseen as stupidly as the caterpillar on the cabbage-leaf, without curiosity or joy or wonder or excitement.' And if that were true seventy years ago, it is even more so today.

MODERN MAN'S ANSWERS

But to return to modern man and his attitude to death, what *does* he believe, assuming one can penetrate this facade of indifference and get an answer at all? Generally there seem to be three answers.

In the first place comes the assertion that at death we 'go out like a light'. There is, of course, a popular slang expression for dying – 'snuffing it' ... disappearing into non-existence like the flame of a candle under a snuffer. The idea is by no means modern. Many a noble pagan philosopher has held it, many an ancient Jew seemed to express death in this way: 'For now I shall lie in the earth; thou wilt seek me, but I shall not be.'[2] The Sadducees of Christ's time taught something very close to this, scorning any idea of a resurrection of the dead. Today, this view, in its more sophisticated form, is widely favoured by those who hold a mechanistic view of the universe.

However, it has some logical weak links. For instance, within a totally evolutionary view of living beings (which is the one generally favoured by mechanistic science), this concept requires a quite arbitrary halt to the process at the point of man's mortality. It assumes that, in a memorable sentence of Leslie Weatherhead's, 'the universe has produced its supreme creation and then flung it away like a capricious child throws away its toy'. It shuts the door dogmatically on any further progress away from the animal and up to the spiritual, as though man in his present form is the highest and best that can ever be – an incredibly arrogant notion.

More than that, it quite arbitrarily rejects all evidence to the contrary. This is essentially unscientific. In terms of true science, the question of life beyond death is an open one. There is a mass of evidence in favour of it (which we shall consider later), but it is an intrinsically unlikely hypothesis. That is to say, the ordinary, day-to-day evidence of our eyes and ears tells us that when a living being dies it remains dead. In a situation like that – where there is evidence for an unlikely hypothesis – it is no sort of answer to dismiss it out of hand. Modern scientific discovery has produced many examples of the unlikeliest hypothesis turning out to be the true one. The mere fact that 'survival' seems unlikely to our materialistic and naturalistic eyes does not by any means disprove it.

Another attitude to death could be described as a diluted Christian one. This consists of a pious optimism expressed in such phrases as 'passed on', 'at rest', and 'at peace'. 'At least she's at peace now', people say of a loved one who has died a lingering and painful death. Much of this popular optimism is perpetuated by the sort of verses one can find in the 'Bereavement' columns of local newspapers. It is, of course, largely sentimental, but it expresses a wide-spread hope, if not belief, that the loved one who has died will be seen again 'in a better place'.

> We miss you more and more each day,
> And wish that you were here.
> But one day we shall meet again
> And wipe away each tear.

It is very easy to ridicule these sentiments and dismiss them as sheer bromides, accepted only because they blunt the pain of separation. The fact is, however, that a dogged, largely uninformed, and even superstitious belief in life beyond the grave hangs on, and these obituary and 'in memoriam' notices in the newspapers are a demonstration of its persistence at the popular 'folk' level.

I called it a diluted Christian view, and that is perhaps being rather generous to it. However, its roots certainly lie in Christian soil, and Christian language is often used to express it.

But the true, biblical doctrine of life after death is far removed from this rather vague and sentimental belief in a future reunion with our dead loved ones, though several very popular Victorian hymns have played their part in perpetuating it:

> What knitting severed friendships up
> Where partings are no more!

Part of this popular piety depends upon the widespread feeling that a benevolent God will, rather like a soft-hearted father, overlook our various faults and moral failures and somehow put it all right 'up there'. No one fails to make the grade for heaven. Nobody is excluded. We speak no ill of the dead, and expect God to do the same. So the popular idea of survival is almost completely deprived of any moral element. Certainly 'judgement' is not generally accepted as part of the survival 'package'. 'He had his faults, of course, but he was a good man at heart,' we say, laying a relative to rest. And we assume that God's standards are no higher than ours, and his charity no less, so the future for the deceased may be regarded with a fair degree of optimism.

But this view is also 'diluted' in another way, in that it is adulterated with materialism. The Christian idea of resurrection is in effect discarded, and in its place is a 'heaven' which is little more than earth with the bumps taken out. The deceased is still 'poor gran' or 'dead dad', and the future reunion is no more than a celestial get-together of the family circle. There is no notion, in the popular mythology, of moral purgation or spiritual transformation. It is simply a move 'upstairs', a second innings.

I do not wish to be too scathing about this attitude,

however. It is far too easy to score points off unsophis-
ticated people who have clung to bits and pieces of
truth that have come their way and fashioned a work-
able and comforting philosophy from them. Much of
the blame – if 'blame' is the right word – should be
placed on the Church, which has generally neglected
the whole subject of life after death and has thus en-
couraged the perpetuation of popular myths and
superstitions.

Not only that, but at the heart of the popular optimism of the people who hold these beliefs there is a
hard kernel of truth. There is life beyond the grave.
'Dear dad' and 'poor gran' have not been annihilated
– or 'snuffed out'. Their memory is worth preserving,
and there are solid grounds for Christian people to
expect to meet their loved ones again. It is not that
popular piety is anti-Christian so much as sub-
Christian. The truth is so much more convincing and
so much more glorious, that it is sad to see simple faith
satisfied with rather tawdry imitations of the real
thing.

The third popular belief about life after death is
not so wide-spread, nor is it so easy to define. It is increasingly to be found among younger people, and
also among a certain kind of intellectual. It is basically
a spiritualistic view, though many of those holding it
would repudiate such an idea violently. It is emphatic
about the finality of bodily death, but agnostic or even
positive about the survival of some element of the
human personality. Many – influenced by Eastern
thought – have gone back to the idea of the soul sur-

viving after death, either permanently or for a period of time. Among them are those who believe in reincarnation. Some have taken a more rationalistic line, and have come to the conclusion that some aspect of 'mind' can survive the death of the body – possibly through the very electrical impulses that record thought and memory.

Heaven, in any recognisable sense, has little place in this scheme of things. The Buddhist 'Nirvana', a shadowy half-life, seems to be the nearest it gets to any notion of a 'place' for the personalities of the dead. Buddha's definition of Nirvana is sometimes quoted with approval: 'Neither a coming nor a going, nor a standing still, nor a falling away, nor a rising up; but it is without fixity, without mobility, without basis ... It is the cessation of becoming.' Such a collection of negatives is a fitting setting for the discarnate personalities which this view of death creates. It is almost as though the destiny of a man is to become a ghost, a shade.

Yet at least those who hold this view are attempting to face the evidence and come to terms with it. It has been born out of many different wombs, including the experience of hallucinogenic drugs, with 'trips' into 'other worlds' of the mind; the new depth psychology, which is concerned to explore inwards into a man's mind and personality; the sheer weight of evidence for some kind of survival of personality after death, and a kind of humanism which is unwilling to accept that man, with all his 'glories', cannot in some form even overcome his final enemy. About the only thing common to all these is a disinclination to allow the physical to become the all-in-all. Slowly a significant group of people – thinking people, at that – is coming around to the view that not only personality, but even existence itself, cannot be explained solely in terms of matter. It is, I suppose, an important step in a new direction for modern man, even if it is only being taken by a minority. And it leads quite logically, of course, to the concept of some kind of human 'survival' of death.

The difference between this view and the prevailing mechanistic one can be seen by contrasting two theories about mind. The prevailing view is that 'mind' and 'brain' are virtually synonymous. The brain – cerebral activity – creates in man what we call 'mind'. But another view is gaining ground, and its supporters would say there is as good evidence for it as there is for the mechanistic view. In this theory, the brain is the vehicle for 'mind', which 'uses' its equipment but cannot be identified with it any more than a driver can be identified with his car. Again the application of this theory to ideas of life after death is fairly obvious.

'Mind' can survive the death of 'brain' – though presumably it would need to find a new vehicle through which to express itself.

THE CHRISTIAN VIEW

At any rate, all of these different views and beliefs about death, and life beyond it, are current today. But there is, of course, another view still held by large numbers of people, which can loosely be termed the 'orthodox Christian view'. For many of us this remains by far the most satisfying and convincing of all the theories and hypotheses being kicked around nowadays. Unlike many of these speculative ideas, the Christian doctrine of life beyond death meets the main criteria of a sound working hypothesis: it fits the known evidence, it provides a satisfactory answer to the problem posed, and it does it without either internal or external contradiction. Rightly understood, it is a magnificently strong and consistent 'system'. In preparing this book, for example, I have not at any point been embarrassed by any detail of the Christian doctrine of resurrection, nor have I found any point at which it raised any problems of inconsistency or contradiction.

It ought to be said, of course, that this only applies to the Christian concept of life beyond death in its full, biblical form. Once parts of it are compromised, inner inconsistencies begin to appear. This is where the Churches have found so much embarrassment over the whole subject of life beyond death. In an attempt to make their traditional doctrines more palatable to naturalistic man, they have often made them totally indigestible.

As will become obvious, I am not advocating a wooden literalism where the Christian doctrine of the 'after-life' is concerned, but simply that the basic beliefs that Christians have held since apostolic times – not the superstitions and popular myths that have become attached to them – are consistent and convincing. As far as possible I have tried to confine myself to those 'basic beliefs' – what the central, orthodox, tradition of Christianity has always held, based on what the Bible clearly teaches. This is not the 'catholic' or 'protestant' or 'evangelical' view of the matter, but what is common to all orthodox Christians. There is plenty of room for difference over details and the application of these beliefs, but they are not central to the argument.

The remainder of this book is taken up with a point by point advocacy of the Christian doctrine of life beyond death, set in the context of modern man and his search for truth, and argued in the light of what we know about that man – his mind, his nature, his spirit, and his needs.

Paterson Smyth, in a book to which I have already referred, and which provided tremendous encouragement and comfort to a war-torn and fearful generation, ended his 'Foreword' with these words: 'This book is a poor, imperfect attempt to put together some of the teachings of our holy religion, to help a troubled world, in the day of its necessity, to look out over the wall.' And so, in a rather different but equally troubled world, is this one.

Notes

[1] Hebrews 9:27.
[2] Job 7:21.

Chapter Two

WHAT HAPPENS WHEN I DIE?

There are many books to tell us what will happen when we leave school, get married, have a baby, or retire from work, but very few indeed to tell us what is likely to happen when an even commoner occurrence comes to us, death. Perhaps it is part of the human conspiracy of silence on the whole subject. Or perhaps it is that we feel there is really nothing to say. If what 'happens' when I die is that I cease to 'happen' any more, then there is little more to be said. Indeed, one of the most brilliant philosophers of the Western world, Wittgenstein, expressed this idea in intensely final terms: 'As in death, too, the world does not change, but ceases. *Death is not an event in life.*'

But for the Christian death is most emphatically an 'event' in life; almost *the* event. It is part of a progress, not the end of the world. The Christian has something to say about dying which goes much further than simply seeing it as the withering away of my world. And what he has to say is highly relevant to every man.

Jung said that a belief in immortality had therapeutic power, because 'no one can live in peace in a house that he knows is shortly to tumble about his ears'. Yet so much naturalistic philosophy and popular 'science' is telling modern man all the time not so much that his 'house' is going to tumble about his ears, but that at a future date it will suddenly cease to exist altogether, and so will the whole world in which he stands. There may be a certain nobility involved in facing that sort of destiny bravely and with dignity, but the concept certainly has little power to bring comfort. When the crutch of belief in immortality is knocked away, the dying man is left to cling to the material world as long as he can, and then slide into oblivion. No wonder he fights and struggles – often with very little dignity at all – to keep a hold, however tenuous, on life. No wonder he sees death as the archenemy, the final, inescapable disaster. And no wonder his life becomes more and more a feverish attempt to avoid not only death itself, but even *thinking* about death.

Yet if there is one thing psychologists and psychiatrists agree about, it is that a healthy attitude to death is absolutely essential if the last decades of life are not to become an appalling and fearful misery. The thoughts of an old person are increasingly taken up with death, and 'indeed it must be so' writes Erastus Evans,[1] 'if the person is to remain psychologically and spiritually healthy . . . Unless the certainty of death is taken clearly into consciousness and faced squarely, it is impossible for the old person to live the last years of life with peace and dignity.' This suggests that modern attempts to ignore death are psychologically damaging, and there would appear to be evidence that this is so.

However, the fact that belief in immortality helps

a man to adjust emotionally to the idea of the inevitability of death is no argument at all for or against the truth of immortality. When most people believed in life after death, an important part of helping people come to terms with death was not to undermine that belief. But now we face a situation in which fewer and fewer people believe in life after death. How are *they* to be helped? Are we to *pretend* that there is 'survival', in order to quieten their fears and give them a few years of bogus hope? There is a new element here, and it calls in question our honesty as well as our compassion. Is there any real comfort in a lie? Can 'faith' be built on deception? And in any case can ourselves, when it is our turn to face death, set aside a life-time of scepticism and swallow a doctrine of immortality which we have rejected since adolescence?

What I am saying is that the crucial question is not 'Does belief in life after death help us to face death?' – it manifestly does – but 'Is it true?' For modern people, shaped by the popular philosophies of the day, there is no other option. We cannot call upon a tribal tradition or an accepted folk-myth which entered our sub-conscious in childhood and has lain there dormant 'until required'. They simply do not exist. We have to face the more difficult, more demanding but also infinitely more rewarding question, 'What is the truth of the matter?' Facing that honestly may well be the preparation we need for facing death honestly. If we decide there is no life beyond, then we can grit our metaphorical teeth and prepare to face with stoical dignity the final extinction of being. But if we decide there *is* life beyond the grave, then the whole business of dying and death assumes a totally different perspective. There is hope: not an illusion, not an induced self-deception, not a conspiracy of friends and relatives to ease our departure, but solid, reliable, trustworthy *hope*.

WHAT HAPPENS TO MY BODY?

So – what happens when I die? And, first of all, what happens to my body?

Medically, the answer is fairly simple – not as simple as it once was, but still a good deal easier than all the other answers concerning death. There are currently three competing definitions of medical death. They have been defined by Dr. Henry Beecher of Harvard[2] as:

1. The moment at which irreversible destruction of brain matter, with no possibility of regaining consciousness, was conclusively determined.

2. The moment at which spontaneous heart beat could not be restored.

3. 'Brain death' as established by the EEG (electro-encephalogram).

In recent years there have been many cases of people who, by older definitions, were 'dead' recovering under treatment. But these are borderline instances. For the most part not only doctors but lay-people too know when a person, or an animal, is 'dead'.

Theologically, death is the disintegration of the body. 'Then the dust returns to the earth as it was' – with its corollary: 'and the spirit returns to God who gave it.'[3] The body, deprived of 'the spirit', has served its purpose. Weary and literally worn out, or brought low by disease, or struck down by 'accident', it 'gives up the ghost' and very soon it has all but disappeared. The moment death comes, disintegration begins. It is as though nature cannot wait to complete its cycle, and recover all the chemical riches which for a lifetime have been stored in the body.

Interestingly, this process has never been regarded by human beings as devaluing humanity. Rather the contrary: funeral rites have served to emphasise the worth and dignity of human life. 'At different times and places the dead bodies of human beings have been honoured in an amazing variety of ways. They have been buried in graves or in tombs or under tumuli or inside pyramids. They have been burnt on pyres, and the ashes have been preserved in urns or have been scattered to the winds. But however diverse man's funerary rites have been, they have all had a common signification. They have signified that a human being has a dignity in virtue of his being human; that his dignity survives his death; and that therefore his dead body must not simply be treated as garbage and be thrown away like the carcase of a dead non-human creature, or like a human being's worn-out boots or clothes.'[4]

So what happens to the body at death is quite simply that it changes from being a living thing to a dead one, and its physical disintegration begins. Of course, in a sense it has already begun, because all our adult lives we are 'dying'; the process of growing old is going on. Death is its crisis, however. We all know that, and it is as well to face it, as bluntly as we can. Whatever hope the Christian faith holds out for the future of personality, it holds out no future at all for the body in which that personality has lived on earth.

A misunderstanding (and, in one case, a mistranslation) of isolated verses in the Bible may in the past have given rise to the idea that *these* bodies will survive death. I am thinking especially of the famous words in Job, immortalised in Handel's *Messiah*: 'I know that my Redeemer lives, and that he shall stand at the latter day upon the earth; and though after my skin worms destroy this body, yet *in my flesh* shall I see God.'[5] That certainly seems quite unambiguous: by a miracle of miracles my disintegrated body will be restored in heaven. In fact, the meaning of the Hebrew original is very unclear – so unclear that the more recent and more reliable Revised Standard Version translates the relevant part in the exactly opposite sense: 'After my skin has been thus destroyed, then *without my flesh* I shall see God.' The concept of immortality is just as clear, but now the 'survival' is not of the earth-bound body, but of another, heavenly one: and this is consistent with the main-stream of the Bible's teaching on death and resurrection.

So at death the body dies. It is discarded, with due reverence, and very soon disintegrates. This leaves the second half of that intriguing sentence in the generally pessimistic book of Ecclesiastes to consider: 'And the spirit returns to God, who gave it.' Here is the rub, the point of departure between those who believe that death is the end of being, and those who believe it is not. Does 'anything' survive death? As the body of John Jones distintegrates, does 'anything' of John Jones remain? And if so, what?

THE GHOST IN THE MACHINE

Let us clear a few preliminary hurdles first of all. For instance, there is this notion of a 'ghost in the human machine', a phrase coined, or at any rate popularised by Gilbert Ryle. The idea behind it is that Christians and others believe that into the physical human frame God 'plants' a 'soul' – the 'ghost in the machine' – which acts as the repository of our moral and spiritual motions, and at death departs from the body and goes back to God (or heaven, or purgatory, or whatever). Ryle and those who think with him, having caricatured the Christian view of man, then proceed to reject the caricature as though it were the real thing.

In fact, so far as I know no serious Christian theologian this century has held such a crude and arbitrary view of the 'soul'. Christians do not subscribe to any view of human nature which divides it into mutually autonomous and independent parts. Man is a whole, a unity: body, mind, and spirit. And man in his totality, the Bible teaches, *is* (not *has* or *contains*) a soul.[6] So various experiments which have been undertaken, such as weighing a human body before and after the moment of death to see if 'anything' were now missing, are completely wrong-headed and even faintly ludicrous. One might as well try to weigh a sense of humour, or a depression, or a passionate love. It speaks volumes for the crude materialism of man that he should for one moment suppose that reality is the same thing as weight or volume. Christians do not believe that there is a 'ghost' in the 'machine', but then they do not believe that man is a machine, either. He is a human being, physically an animal, spiritually a 'little lower than the angels'.[7] The whole person is more than simply his physique, and may well survive the death of his outward form, without being described as a 'ghost'. But we shall return to that shortly.

As a second hurdle, we must say that the area of life beyond is an area of faith. We can test our beliefs against known facts, but short of dying ourselves we shall never be able to 'prove' them. What I propose to do is to state the Christian view (as I understand it) and then, in later chapters, to test that view as rigorously as I can in order to demonstrate its consistency and rationality. No one can do more than that, honestly; and no one can fairly ask for more than that, either.

WHAT IS MAN?

The third hurdle is really a very big one, and concerns the nature of man. If we are to ask what happens to John Jones when he dies, then we need to be quite clear as to who and what John Jones is. This is one of the great arguments of the twentieth century. Is man

an animal? Is he a machine? Or is he more than either
or both of them? Obviously Christians, who believe
that God 'made man in his own image',[8] must ada-
mantly maintain that he is more than an animal, and
certainly more than a machine. But we need to ask, in
what way is he 'more'?

There are many things that distinguish man from
the animals, and it may be worth listing some of them.
Man uses tools, man uses language, man has art and
music, man has a religious instinct, man is conscious
of his own being, man can rise above his instincts, man
is aware of his own mortality, man has a moral sense
and deals in the realm of such abstract concepts as
justice, love, forgiveness, compassion, sympathy,
generosity and kindness. Man, in short, is *personal*. He
has a personality and he is a person. Without pressing
those definitions, we know at heart what they mean.

Equally, of course, there are many ways in which
man is linked with the animals: his anatomy, his
senses, his appetites, his natural instincts, his
physiology, his method of reproduction – all of these
he shares with the animals. There is no need for
Christians to be defensive here. Homo Sapiens is
closely linked with, and may well have evolved from,
the animals. But that is not to say that he is nothing
else.

For that matter, man has many machine-like qualities. His limbs are perfect examples of engineering,
his brain is a superb computer, his eyes are the finest
cameras yet devised. But he is more than a machine.

And the 'plus' is the personal, the thing that not

only distinguishes a man from a machine or an animal, but even distinguishes him from another man. All of those personal attributes – art, music, abstract concepts, self-awareness – are distinctive to man among the creatures. And these qualities, unlike his 'animal' body, are manifestly 'immortal'. Beethoven dies, but the Ninth Symphony plays on. John Jones dies, but the love and generosity and kindness in which he shared live on. There can be no doubt, at this level at least, that 'something' survives death, and the 'something' that does is linked with the element of personality rather than the body.

So far few would disagree. But all of that falls far short of the Christian belief, which is that *personality* survives death: not just elements of it, or memories of it, but the whole person. The *real* John Jones – the thing that distinguishes him from Robert Brown, the distinctively personal 'him' – cannot die, and does not die. And, once again, we shall be returning to that subject later on.

What needs to be established at this stage is that man – the whole human being – is a personality in a bodily form, but that the bodily form is not the personality. True, John Jones has fair hair and blue eyes – but look at that verb! He 'has' them. They 'belong' to him. But they, and all the other parts of his physical body, do not add up to a 'person'. We should never describe his 'personality' in those terms. The real John Jones, the one who loves his wife and enjoys sunsets and growing roses, is so much more than a computer linked to a machine. He is a person, and that is another way of saying he is a 'soul'. And it is the *person* of John Jones that survives his death, not as a fleeting spirit or emanation, but as a man.

There is quite an argument in the scientific realm, as I have indicated, between those who believe that brain is mind, and those who believe that mind uses brain. Once accept the second concept, and it becomes completely rational to go on and say that mind survives the death of the brain – provided it can have a new 'vehicle' for its activity. Personality is clearly connected more with the mind than the body (though it is hard for us to conceive of personality *without* a body – as in the Christian doctrine of God, for example), and if 'mind' survives death there is very little difficulty in accepting that personality survives death, too.

The question then becomes, in what form does the personality of John Jones express itself after death? Professor D. M. Mackay of Keele University is one of Britain's foremost experts in the communications systems of the human brain. He also believes, as a Christian, in immortality. Here is how he sees it: 'It is not as disembodied spirits that God promises us eternal life, but as personalities expressed in a new kind of body – what the apostle Paul calls a "spiritual body". Just as a message is still the same message, whether it's spoken in words or flashed in morse code, so, according to the Bible, we shall be the same persons, whatever the material form in which our personalities may be expressed. Nothing' – he adds – 'in the scientific picture of man, however complete it may one day become, could affect the truth of this doctrine one way or the other.'[9]

He sees personality as a 'message', and our present bodies as one means of 'transmitting' that message. But like all Christians he looks on to 'a new kind of body' – a better 'transmitter' – in a new kind of life beyond death.

This is precisely what the Bible itself teaches and, as he so trenchantly asserts, there is nothing science can say against it. It is not intrinsically irrational, as some would claim; nor, of course, can it be rationally proved as some would wish. One can only assert that the survival of personality is what Christianity teaches, that this personality expresses itself in the 'life beyond' in a new form suited to its new environment; and that this doctrine fits the available facts and answers the ultimate questions at least as well as, and probably a great deal better than, any theory man has yet devised.

So, where have we arrived? When I die, my body disintegrates, but my personality – the 'real' me – lives on; this personality is going to express itself in the 'life beyond' in a totally different kind of 'body'. That, I have said, is the Christian position. In following chapters I shall try to justify that assertion; and then, in rather more detail, attempt to answer the question, 'What kind of a "totally different" body?' But first I would like to consider the whole question of the survival of the personality after death.

NOTES

1 SCM Press.
2 In a lecture reported in *The Times*, December 12th, 1967.
3 Ecclesiastes 12 : 7.
4 Arnold Toynbee, in *Man's Concern with Death*, Hodder.
5 Job 19 : 25–27.
6 Genesis 2 : 7.
7 Psalm 8.
8 Genesis 1 : 27.
9 In an essay in *Inter-Varsity*, 1970

Chapter Three

EVIDENCES FOR SURVIVAL

The evidence *against* survival is simply expressed: it is the evidence of our own eyes. When a person dies, they have 'gone'. However we express it, we regard their 'life' as ended. We talk about the 'departed' – or used to. Not only that, but we are familiar with death in so many other realms too. Plants, fish, and animals die, and in every case death is the 'end'. You may preserve their form but the life is gone.

In the nature of things, therefore, the evidence for survival is not so simply expressed. It has to overcome the apparently overwhelming evidence of our senses. And to introduce into it a concept which distinguishes between body and personality is to make the issue even more difficult.

Yet the fact is that the evidence is very strong. So strong that Dr. John Beloff writing in *The Humanist* magazine in 1965 argued very persuasively that, rather than try to deny 'survival', Humanists should accept that it probably occurs and look for a more 'rational' explanation than that offered by religion. He suggested a theory based on the electrical impulses or 'waves' produced by the human brain, which might continue functioning for some time – years perhaps – after death. But the point is that he felt it necessary to find a theory to explain a phenomenon which he accepted as more or less undeniable, and which might 'one day present a challenge to Humanism as profound in its own way as that which Darwinian Evolution did to Christianity a century ago'. The evidence for the paranormal points, he wrote, to a 'dualistic world where mind or spirit has an existence separate from the world of material things'. Humanists 'cannot afford to close our minds . . . to the possibility of some kind of survival whether in a discarnate or reincarnate form'.

What is this evidence for survival, and where does it come from? Those who suppose that it springs mainly from ghost stories and spiritualistic seances are rather out of date. The last century, and especially since the foundation of the Society for Psychical Research, has seen the amassing of an enormous amount of carefully documented evidence on the subject. It does not follow that all of this evidence is equally relevant, and some of it may even be misleading, but it cannot be ignored. Contrary to popular opinion, the SPR is not concerned solely with so-called 'spiritualistic' phenomena; its members include people who are agnostic about survival, as well as some who are convinced supernaturalists. Its brief is to investigate in a scientific and controlled way any and all psychic manifestations, and over a period of years it has documented a vast amount of material relating to death and life after death.

SPIRITUALISM AND OTHER PARANORMAL EXPERIENCES

Let me say right away that very clearly a good deal of what is called 'spiritualism' is highly unspiritual. Much of it is fraudulent, or based on a combination of wishful thinking and hallucination. Let me also say that so far as I am concerned the practice of attempting to communicate with the dead through mediums is wrong and harmful, and is specifically forbidden in the Bible.[1] But, whatever the motivation and however undesirable the means, there undoubtedly exists a body of well-documented phenomena associated with 'spiritualism' which strongly suggests (to put it mildly) that human personality is not always extinguished at death.

Some years ago I met a young man who had recently become a Christian. Edward Atkinson had for twelve years previously been a convinced and active spiritualist, and one of the founders of the Young Spiritualist Council. His conversion was a painful and costly affair. He had frequently and publicly attacked Christianity, and on one fateful day, in his own words, 'scornfully challenged the miserable carpenter who called himself God to invade, crush and re-make *me*'. And he did. In November 1961 Edward Atkinson left the spiritualist movement. But the faculty of clairvoyance only left him fifteen months later, and he was in the intervening period the subject of constant attack by spirits. Eventually, overcome by the reality of Christ in his life, they left him, and with them went his malign gift of clairvoyance.

The significance of his story is this. Although he has spent much of his time subsequently warning Christians of the dangers of spiritualism, Edward Atkinson has never had any doubts at all about the reality of his earlier spiritualistic experiences or that he had in fact communicated with the discarnate spirits of the dead.[2]

The shadowy world of the 'spirits', from which discarnate 'voices' bring 'messages' to their loved ones on earth, is far removed from the heaven described by the Bible. I do not profess to know why some people after death seem able to communicate with living people through mediums, but I do not envy either them or the recipients of their messages. There is a better thing than this beyond the grave – but even saying that does not silence the testimony of these 'spirits' to the reality of 'survival'.

However, it is not the testimony of spiritualism that I am concerned with, except as an incidental factor. The SPR has also documented many other far more revealing and convincing incidents relating to death and the human personality. One of them is so relevant to this argument, and so well documented, that I shall reproduce it in full.[3] The late Lord Geddes wrote:

On Saturday, November 9th, a few minutes after midnight, I began to feel very ill and by 2 o'clock was definitely suffering from acute gastro-enteritis. ... By 10 o'clock I had developed all the symptoms of very acute poisoning ... pulse and respirations being quite impossible to count. I realised I was very ill and very quickly reviewed my whole financial position . . . thereafter at no time did my consciousness appear to me to be in any way dimmed, but suddenly realised that *my* consciousness was separating from another consciousness which was also me. These for purposes of description we could call the A and B consciousness, and throughout what follows the ego attached itself to the A consciousness. The B personality I recognised as belonging to the body, and as my physical condition grew worse . . . I realised that [it] was beginning to show signs of being composite, that is, built up of 'consciousness' from the head, heart, viscera, etc. The components became more individual and the B consciousness began to disintegrate, while the A consciousness, which was now me, seemed to be altogether outside the body, which it could see. Gradually I realised that I could see not only my body and the bed in which it was, but everything in the whole house and garden, and then I realised that I was not only seeing 'things' at home, but in London and in Scotland, in fact wherever my attention was directed it seemed to me; and the explanation I received, from what source I do not know, but which I found myself calling my mentor, was that I was free in a time dimension of space, wherein 'now' was in some way equivalent to 'here' in the ordinary three dimensional space of everyday life. I next realised that my vision included not only 'things' in the ordinary three dimensional world, but also 'things' in these four and more dimensional places that I was in. From now on the description is and must be entirely metaphorical because there are no words which really describe what I saw or rather appreciated. Although I had no body I had what appeared to be perfect two-eyed vision, and what I saw can only be described in this way, that I was conscious of a psychic stream flowing with life through time, and this gave me the impression of being visible, and it seemed to me to have a particularly intense iridescence. I understood from my mentor that all our brains are just end-organs projecting as it were from the three dimensional universe into the psychic stream and flowing with it into the fourth and fifth dimensions. Around each brain, as I saw it, there seemed to be what I can only describe in ordinary words as a condensation of the psychic stream . . . I saw A enter the bedroom. I realised she got a terrible shock and I saw her hurry to the telephone; I saw my doctor leave his patients and come very quickly, and heard him say, or saw him think, 'He is nearly gone.' I heard him quite clearly speaking to me on the bed, but I was not in touch with the body and could not answer him. I was really cross when he took a syringe and rapidly injected my body with something, which I afterwards learned was camphor. As the heart began to beat more strongly I was drawn back and I was intensely annoyed because I was so interested and just beginning to understand where I was and what I was 'seeing'. . . . Once I was back all the clarity of vision of anything and everything disappeared and I was just possessed of a glimmer of consciousness which was suffused with pain.

It is surprising to note that this dream, vision or experience has shown no tendency to fade like a dream would fade, nor has it shown any tendency that I am aware of to grow or to rationalise itself as a dream would do. I think that the whole thing simply means that but for medical treatment of a peculiarly prompt and vigorous kind I was dead to the three dimensional universe. If this is so and if in fact the experience of liberation of consciousness in the fourth dimensional universe is not imagination, it is a most important matter to place on record. . . .

This account is only one of a number which have the same characteristics – a division, in the face of death, between body and 'personality'. This division is very vivid to the reporters, but not at all terrifying or disturbing. Generally they record their reluctance to return to their bodies and re-enter 'normal' life.

A more recent and very remarkable case is that of Edmund Wilbourne, a captain in the Church Army. His story was first made public on BBC Radio Merseyside in 1976, but it relates events that took place 27 years earlier and were medically documented then. Captain Wilbourne's reluctance to publicise his astonishing experience is perhaps the most convincing argument for its authenticity.

He was critically ill in Crumpsall Hospital, near Manchester, with pleurisy and pneumonia. He died, and was in fact certified dead and his body 'laid out' by a nurse. At that point he seemed to leave his body, and could actually observe the nurse shaving and preparing his body for the mortuary. He felt linked to the body on the bed by a cord, but then the cord was severed and he arrived at a 'place' which he took to be heaven. It was, in his own words, 'nothing like floating on clouds or harps or anything of that sort,' but a place of activity and meaning. 'I felt more alive and more alert than I've ever done since.'

Then he saw Jesus Christ, recognising him by the print of the nails in his hands and his feet – as he thought at the time, they were 'the only man-made things in heaven'. He recognised other people, too, friends who had died, and was not at all pleased when an insistent voice grew louder and louder, praying, 'O God, don't let him die, he's got work to do for you.' Finally, as he explains, 'the Lord Jesus turned me round on my shoulder and gave me a gentle push, saying something to the effect, "It's not time for you yet."' Captain Wilbourne came round, two hours after his 'death', in the hospital mortuary.

Subsequently, in an interview in a book,[4] he expanded on his experience of 'heaven'. He described it as a place of intense light and activity, with Jesus 'light itself' – and yet emphatically a 'person', in the same way as the other people he recognised: his Sunday school teacher, his mother and grandmother, and his doctor, who had died just previously. 'They did have physical shape,' he recalls, 'but it somehow combined the youth and vigour of a twenty-one year old with a sense of perfect maturity.'

This account by Edmund Wilbourne has been paralleled in the experience of many others, though often less vividly. Certainly his description of a place of intense light beyond death is repeated over and over again in the accounts of people who have had similar experiences and so, as we have seen, is this sense of separation of spirit from body at, or near, death.

I do not know how much weight one should attach to this kind of thing. It is not 'scientific' evidence, of course, as it is a non-verifiable record of an individual's private interior experiences. However, when many sane and balanced people, over a long period of time but in roughly similar circumstances, record substantially the same experience, one must attach some weight to it. Certainly Lord Geddes, a very distinguished physician and professor of anatomy, would not seem to be the kind of person to indulge in fanciful make-believe about so important a topic.

A mountaineer has recorded a rather similar experience, not during the crisis of an illness, but during the few moments when he slipped over the edge of a precipice, hung some twenty feet over the edge on the end of a rope, and faced sudden death. His account is less scientific, but just as interesting.[5]

I found myself hanging on the rope a few feet below the crest of the ridge. I turned, snatched at the rocks and clawed my way back. I had fallen altogether about 20 feet and the rope . . . had held . . .

During the time I was doing this a curious rigidity or tension gripped my whole being, mental and physical ... It was an overwhelming sensation and quite outside my experience. It was as though all life's forces were in process of undergoing some fundamental evolutionary change, the change called death ... I know now that death is not to be feared, it is a supreme experience, the climax, not the anti-climax of life.

For how long I experienced this crescendo of power I cannot say, time no longer existed as time ... Then suddenly this feeling was superseded by a feeling of complete indifference and detachment, detachment as to what was happening or likely to happen to that body. I seemed to stand aside from my body. I was not falling for the reason that I was not in a dimension where it was possible to fall. I, that is, my consciousness, was apart from my body and not in the least concerned with what was befalling it.

Commenting on this experience, the author says, 'It is not within my province to discuss that which only death can prove; yet to me this experience was a convincing one, it convinced me that consciousness survives beyond the grave.'

Two further instances, both well documented and with all the marks of authenticity, seem to support that conclusion. The first is from the First World War, and concerns an apparition reported *before* the percipient knew of his friend's death.

The percipient was Lieut. J. J. Larkin, of the R.A.F. and the apparition was that of one of Lieut.

Larkin's fellow officers, Lieut. David M'Connel, killed in an airplane crash on December 7th, 1918. Lieut. Larkin reported that he spent the afternoon of December 7th in his room at the barracks. He sat in front of the fire reading and writing and was wide awake all the time. At about 3.30 p.m. he heard someone walking up the passage.

'The door opened with the usual noise and clatter which David always made: I heard his "Hello Boy!" and I turned half round in my chair and saw him standing in the doorway, half in and half out of the room holding the door knob in his hand. He was dressed in his full flying clothes, but wearing his naval cap, there being nothing unusual in his appearance ... I remarked "Hello! back already?" He replied, "Yes, got there all right, had a good trip" ... I was looking at him at the time he was speaking. He said, "Well, Cheerio!", closed the door noisily and went out.'

Shortly after this a friend dropped in to see Lieut. Larkin and Larkin told him that he had just seen and talked to Lieut. M'Connel. [This friend sent a corroborative statement to the Society for Psychical Research.] Later on that day it was learned that Lieut. M'Connel had been instantly killed in a flying accident which occurred at about 3.25 p.m. Mistaken identity seems to be ruled out, since the light was very good in the room where the apparition appeared. Moreover, there was no other man in the barracks at the time who in any way resembled Lieut. M'Connel. It was also found that he was wearing his naval cap when he was killed, apparently an unusual circumstance. Agent and percipient had been 'Very good friends, though not intimate friends in the true sense of the world.'[6]

The second instance, the Chaffin Will Case, has become famous. As Rosalind Heywood remarks, 'Whatever the explanation, there is *something* to be explained.'

James Chaffin, a farmer in North Carolina, died in 1921 as the result of a fall, leaving a widow and two sons. In 1905 he made a will leaving his whole property to his third son, Marshall, who proved the will and himself died about a year later, leaving a widow and a son, a minor. In June 1925 the second son, James, began to have vivid dreams of his father appearing at his bedside and speaking. This vision may have been a 'borderland' experience, occurring between sleeping and waking. It was more realistic than pure dreams usually are but in an experience as informative as this the distinction is of little importance.

The figure was dressed in a black overcoat which James had often seen his father wearing. [James said that] 'He took hold of his overcoat this way and pulled it back and said "You will find my will in my overcoat pocket" and then disappeared.'

James went to his elder brother's house and found the coat, and inside the inner pocket, which was sewn up, a roll of paper with the words, 'read the

27th chapter of Genesis in my daddie's old Bible.'
James found the old Bible in a drawer in his
mother's house and in the presence of witnesses
found between two folded pages on which the 27th
chapter of Genesis was printed, another will, dated
January 16th, 1919, whereby the Testator, 'after
reading the 27th Chapter of Genesis,' in which the
supplanting of Esau by Jacob is related, divided his
property equally between his four sons, and added,
'You must all take care of your Mammy.'

The second will, though unattested by witnesses,
was valid by the law of the State . . . Before probate,
however, the Testator appeared again to his son,
James, saying: 'Where is my old will?' and showing
'considerable temper'.'

These instances, like earlier ones, are cited in
Rosalind Heywood's contribution to the symposium
Man's Concern with Death. She quotes the views of
three distinguished scholars, none of them in any way
committed to a 'survivalist' position.

First, the well-known American psychologist, Professor Gardner Murphy.

Where then do I stand? To this the reply is: what
happens when an irresistible force strikes an im-
movable object? To me the evidence cannot be by-
passed, nor, on the other hand, can conviction be
achieved . . . Trained as a psychologist and now in
my sixties, I do not actually anticipate finding myself
in existence after physical death. If this is the answer

the reader wants, he can have it. But if this means that in a serious philosophical argument I would plead the anti-survival case, the conclusion is erroneous. I linger because I cannot cross the stream. We need far more evidence; we need new perspectives; perhaps we need more courageous minds. (*Challenge of Psychical Research*, Harpers, New York, 1961.)

Next, the doyen of British psychologists, Professor Sir Cyril Burt.

The uncertainty leaves the matter open in *both* directions. On the one hand the theoretical psychologist (and that includes the para-psychologist) should, on this particular issue, preserve a strict agnosticism, pressing physicalistic interpretations as far as they will go, and, even if in the end he feels compelled to adopt the hypothesis of a surviving mind, he must remember that it is, like the ether of old, no more than a hypothesis. On the other hand, those who, from reasons of faith, metaphysics, or what they take to be personal revelation, still wish to believe in survival for themselves or those they love, need have no grounds for fearing scientific censure. Thus our verdict on the whole matter must be the same as that pronounced by Plato two thousand years ago – the reply he puts into the mouth of Socrates while waiting to drink the hemlock. 'I would not positively assert that I shall join the company of those good men who have already departed from this life; but I cherish a good hope.' Hope implies, not the virtual certainty of success but the possibility of success. And it is, I think, one important result of recent psychological and para-psychological investigations to have demonstrated, in the face of the confident denials of the materialists and the behaviourists, *at least the possibility* of survival in some form or other, though not necessarily in the form depicted by traditional piety or fourth century metaphysics. (In a symposium *Science & ESP*, Routledge and Kegan Paul.)

And finally, Professor C. D. Broad, sometime Knightbridge Professor of Moral Philosophy at Cambridge. He incidentally, does not hide the fact he does not want to survive.

The position as I see it is this. In the known relevant normal and abnormal facts there is nothing to suggest and much to counter-suggest, the possibility of any kind of persistence of the psychical aspect of a human being after the death of his body. On the other hand, there are many quite well attested *paranormal* phenomena which strongly suggest the full-blown survival of a human personality. *Most people manage to turn a blind eye to one or other of these two relevant sets of data, but it is part of the business of a professional philosopher to try to envisage steadily both of them together. The result is naturally a state of hesitation and scepticism*[8] (in the correct as opposed to the popular sense of that word). I think I may say that for my part I should be slightly more annoyed than surprised if I should find myself in some sense persisting immediately after the death of my present body. One can only wait and see, or alternatively (which is no less likely) wait and not see. (*Lectures on Psychical Research*, Routledge and Kegan Paul, 1962.)

THE RESURRECTION OF JESUS

However, none of these pieces of evidence, nor all of them taken together, is as full, as convincing, and as consistent as the best-documented 'survival' of all time, the resurrection of Jesus. Undoubtedly this must have extensive consideration in any book on this subject, whatever one's personal beliefs or convictions about Jesus Christ, if only because so much has been placed upon it and so much depends upon it. It has been exhaustively studied, both by protagonists and antagonists, and is rightly reckoned to be the absolute lynch-pin of the Christian position on life after death. Even the apostle Paul saw it that way: 'If Christ has not been raised,' he wrote, 'your faith is futile and you are still in your sins.'[9]

On the other hand, the resurrection of Christ is not 'typical'. He claimed to be the Son of God. 'It was not possible for him to be held . . . by the pangs of death,' the apostle Peter told the awe-struck crowds at Pentecost.[10] In his case, the body did not disintegrate, but was instantly transformed, leaving behind an empty tomb. This is not the path ordinary humans are called to walk; or rather, this is not the pace at which we are called to walk it. In the resurrection event – and the 'ascension', when the body of Jesus Christ returned to heaven – events which 'normally' take enormous periods of time are telescoped into a few days.

Yet in other ways it is entirely typical, and is clearly intended to be: 'In fact Christ has been raised from the dead, the *first fruits* of those who have fallen asleep.'[11] He is the beginning of a 'harvest' of resurrections, and in that sense is the pacemaker and the prototype.

So let us look at the resurrection of Christ, to see what it does, and what it does not say about the more general question of life beyond death. There are several far more exhaustive treatments of the subject, and these are recommended to those who would wish to pursue the details and tie up all the ends.[12] In my treatment I shall restrict myself to the 'irreducible minimum' of what seems to me to be the heart of the matter.

Few people nowadays – and none at all who are taken seriously, I think – would deny that there was a man called Jesus who lived in Judaea in the early years of the first century AD. His existence is not only attested by the Gospel writers (who might be considered pre-judiced witnesses) but also by a number of distin-guished secular or non-Christian historians – including the Roman Tacitus, and the Jew, Josephus. There is also an abundance of archaeological material showing how far and how fast Christianity – belief in this same Jesus as the Son of God – had spread by about AD 70. In other words, in a single life-time a man was born, lived, died, and became the founder of a major religion which held that he rose from the dead. This was not a peripheral belief about Jesus, something his followers could accept or reject as secondary. It *was* their message – 'Jesus and the resurrection.'[13]

Let us be absolutely clear what this means. Within the life-time of those who were eye-witnesses of the crucial events a major religion was born and spread with amazing rapidity which claimed that its founder, executed by the Roman authorities, had risen from the dead. No amount of argument over details about the crucifixion and burial of Christ can obscure this. *They* believed it – his contemporaries and his opponents, including the authorities who executed him, who were desperate to disprove the Christian case but were manifestly unable to do so. Unlike us, they had access to eye-witnesses. They could cross-examine them, and probe for flaws. Given the will to do so, it should not have been difficult to demolish so incredible an argument as that a man had risen from the dead. *And the will existed*, yet it was not done. One can only deduce that it simply could not be done.

It is sometimes said that those were gullible days, quite unlike our modern world; that people then were predisposed to believe all manner of weird and wonderful legends and fantasies. But this simply will not hold water. The first century was an age of cynicism and rationalism. The dominant Greek school of thought, Stoicism, did not believe in any kind of life after death. Neither did one of the two major Jewish theological groupings, the Sadducees. Thus there was no shortage of eloquent and learned voices to do battle against any religion or philosophy proposing as its central belief that a man rose from the dead. The re-action of the Greek Areopagus – a philosophical coun-cil – to Paul's message of resurrection is proof enough of that. They listened to him attentively until he spoke of Jesus being raised from the dead, but then the meet-ing broke up. This was the point of no return. Far from being gullibly disposed to accept it, they behaved exactly like their twentieth-century counterparts and mocked the very idea.[14]

So, from two assertions which are very nearly un-deniable – that Jesus of Nazareth existed as an histori-cal character in the first thirty or so years of the first century AD, and that by AD 70 the Christian religion was well established in the Graeco-Roman world – we are able to argue the strength of the case for the resur-rection of Jesus. Those who care to refute it have got to face these facts head on, and find an explanation for them that is easier to believe than that Jesus rose from the dead. So far nobody has done it.

Of course, the 'case' for the resurrection of Jesus goes further than that. Any man who lives has to die, so it is easy to believe that Jesus died, too. And it is historically consistent that he should have been 'cruci-fied under Pontius Pilate' – the Roman Governor of Judaea at the time. Incidentally, we now have archae-ological proof that Pilate actually existed – something earlier ages have lacked.

But on the third day after his death – the first 'Easter Sunday' – his disciples discovered his tomb to be empty. That empty tomb is an important piece of evidence.

After all, the burials of executed public agitators like
Jesus are not hole-in-the-corner affairs. There had been
talk earlier that he would 'rise from the dead', so obviously the authorities would take special care to see
that he did not. We are told in the Gospels of a guard
on the tomb, and of the sepulchre itself being sealed.
But his disciples found that the tomb was empty, and
within a few weeks were saying so publicly. Yet so far
as history records, the authorities offered no counter to
this remarkable claim. They did not produce the body
of Jesus. They did not even produce the guards to say
they had been attacked and the body stolen – though
the idea was put up at one stage. The only recorded
explanation offered by the anti-Christian parties was
that this and all the miracles of Jesus were demonic in
origin.[15]

But it was not just that the disciples found the tomb
of Jesus empty. A number of them actually *saw* him,
alive and vocal. Later all the disciples saw him – indeed, according to Paul, 'more than five hundred saw
him at once'.[16] Not only that, but he adds 'most of
whom are still alive'. That is the statement of a man
confident of the truth of his evidence. Look, he says in
effect, here is the proof that Jesus rose from the dead.
He was seen at different times and places by all the
twelve apostles, and then on one occasion by five
hundred people . . . and if you don't believe me, you
can check it for yourself, because most of them are still
alive. As Paul wrote those words to the church at
Corinth, some time before AD 70, he was inviting
sceptics to put his claim to the test. There were

hundreds of eye-witnesses of the resurrection. True, they were a few hundred miles away in Judaea, but they were not inaccessible. Paul was presenting Christianity as it ought always to be presented – as an historical religion, rooted in certain events that actually happened at a place in geography and a point in history.

NOTES

[1] e.g. Leviticus 19: 31; Deuteronomy 18: 11.
[2] His story was related by himself in *Crusade*, September, 1964.
[3] An address by the late Lord Geddes to the Royal Medical Society in Edinburgh, 1937, quoted by Rosalind Heywood in *Man's Concern with Death*, Hodder.
[4] *Invitation to Healing* by Roy Lawrence, Kingsway.
[5] F. S. Smythe. *The Spirit of the Hills*, Hodder, 1935.
[6] Summarised by Professor Gardner Murphy in *Three Papers on the Survival Problem*, American Society for Psychical Research, 1945.
[7] W. H. Salter, *Zoar*, or *The Evidence of Psychical Research concerning Survival*, Sidgwick and Jackson, 1961.
[8] My italics.
[9] 1 Corinthians 15: 17.
[10] Acts 2: 24.
[11] 1 Corinthians 15: 20.
[12] e.g. *The Evidence for the Resurrection* by J. N. D. Anderson, IVP.
[13] Acts 17: 18.

[14] Acts 17 : 30–32.
[15] See *Beyond the Gospels*, R. Dunkerley, Penguin.
[16] 1 Corinthians 15 : 6.

Chapter Four

WHAT KIND OF BODY?

What was it that these Christian eye-witnesses of the resurrection saw? It is an important question, highly relevant to our investigation of life beyond death. It is not enough to say that they saw, or met, 'Jesus'. In what form did they see or meet him? Was he exactly the same in every way as before his death? If not, in what way had he changed?

Perhaps the simplest way to answer that is to draw up two lists, one of the dissimilarities between the pre- and post-resurrection Christs, and the other of the similarities.

Into the first list – the negative one – must go a number of pieces of eye-witness evidence which are frequently overlooked, or else seized upon to support a pre-conceived notion of the nature of Jesus after the resurrection. For example, it is really quite undeniable that the appearance of Jesus was changed, and changed to such an extent or in such a way that even his closest friends failed to recognise him. Mary of Magdala 'supposed he was the gardener'[1] on the morning of the resurrection. Two disciples walked seven miles to Emmaus with him the same day and did not recognise him until a familiar mannerism connected with giving thanks for the evening meal 'opened their eyes'.[2] Less obviously, Peter and the other disciples needed – and received – other evidence than the evidence of sight that it was in fact Jesus who met them during their fishing expedition on the Sea of Tiberias. This incident is in some ways the most revealing of them all.[3]

After the resurrection – and apparently slightly impatient at the delay in bringing in 'the kingdom' which they were expecting – seven of the disciples took a boat out on this inland sea for a night's fishing. But despite their professional skills, they caught absolutely nothing. However, 'just as day was breaking' Jesus stood on the beach and called to them. 'The disciples did not know that it was Jesus.' He told them to cast their net on the starboard side of the boat. They did, and caught an enormous quantity of fish. John then shouted to Peter 'It's the Lord!' and Peter, typically, leapt overboard and swam ashore to greet him. When the others followed, Jesus had lit a fire on the beach and they all had breakfast together. At this point John observes, 'Now none of the disciples dared ask him, "who are you?" They knew it was the Lord.' Now obviously it was not the sense of sight that gave them this knowledge, or they would not have even thought of asking 'Who are you?' It was the miracle he had done, and the personality they knew so well, that convinced them that it was Christ they were meeting.

But it was not simply that the external appearance of Jesus was changed. The physical properties of his body were also changed, and very radically indeed. Although he specifically denied that he was a ghost or spirit[4] (and clearly he was not, because he could be touched, and he was able to prepare and eat a meal) and although he had 'flesh and bones', as the disciples could see,[5] yet he was able to enter rooms through locked doors,[6] appear in places many miles apart without apparently travelling by any recognised means, and eventually be 'taken from their sight' on the Mount of the Ascension.[7] It is hardly necessary to say that none of these things is feasible for a human body, and in fact none of these things happened to Jesus during his earthly life. Before the resurrection his body was unquestionably that of a normal human being. If he did not eat, he got hungry. If he did not drink, he was thirsty. At night he was tired and needed to sleep. If he was cut, he bled. The long journey from Galilee to Jerusalem took weeks, perhaps months, and there was never the slightest suggestion that he might travel it in any but a completely 'normal' way.

Yet *after* the resurrection all this was changed.

Quite obviously Paul was right when he claimed that 'Christ being raised from the dead, will never die again; death has no longer dominion over him.'[8] That in itself says something very remarkable about the body of Jesus after his resurrection. All human bodies are mortal. They lie under the 'dominion' of death. Or, to put it in more usual language, they begin to die from the moment they are born. But this new body of Jesus was not subject either to the sudden onslaught of disease or accident, nor to the insidious and irresistible process of growing old.

And this body was not confined within the limits of

our space–time world. It simply could not have been composed as 'ordinary' bodies are. It may indeed have had 'flesh and bones', but it was not limited by them in the way we are. Bars and bolts could not shut it out, and death itself could not touch it. It was a *real* body, there can be no doubt about that. Hundreds of people could not have been so mistaken, especially when Jesus offered clear evidence of it. But it was not an earthbound body. It was something that bore a developmental relationship to an earthly human body, but it was not identical with it. There was clearly a continuity of life between the body of Jesus and the body of the resurrected Jesus, but in the process of resurrection it had undergone a very fundamental change. That, at least, seems obvious.

So much for the list of dissimilarities: the body of Jesus after the resurrection had a different appearance and also a different 'form'. It was 'like' the previous body, it had some sort of developmental relationship to it, but it was obviously not 'identical' with it.

Now we must consider the similarities. Strangely, they all came down to one factor, but that factor is so important that it outweighs all the dissimilarities. It is simply this: Jesus before and after the resurrection was undeniably *the same person*. No matter what extraordinary changes had taken place in his bodily form, all who knew him well had no doubt at all who he was. They 'knew' it was the Lord.

Let us see *how* they recognised him. Mary of Magdala recognised his voice – or, possibly, a familiar mode of address: the way he said 'Mary'. The two on the road to Emmaus recognised his mannerisms: the way he broke bread. The disciples by the lake recognised his characteristic activity in the way he performed the miracle of the fish. More than that, of course, they recognised his characteristic thoughtfulness in lighting the fire and preparing breakfast. In other words they all recognised the person, or the personality, of a man they had known well, and were so sure it was him that they were prepared to die for that belief, as many of his early followers did.

What we arrive at, then, in examining the resurrection of Jesus is exactly what we found in all the other 'evidences' of survival: essentially what 'survived' death was his personality. But in this case an earlier supposition – that this surviving personality would need a new bodily vehicle in which to express itself – becomes a fact. The personality of Jesus after his resurrection from death expressed itself in a new body, no longer subject to the limitations imposed on a space-time, earthly body. The 'message' was the same – to use Professor Mackay's illustration quoted earlier – but the 'transmitter' was new and better. Not only was it better, in general terms (less confined, less limited, immortal) but it was also perfectly designed to live *on* in a spiritual environment. It was no longer really at home in this world.

THE TRANSFORMATION OF OUR BODIES

And this is the pattern, according to the Bible, for all resurrection. Not immediately at death, as in the case of Jesus, but just as instantly our bodies will be changed, and we shall enter a new environment in a form perfectly suited to life there. And it will be *us*: not our ghosts, not our 'souls', but the whole personality will break through the barrier of flesh and on into a new realm of living, just as it did with Jesus. The apostle Paul puts it very dramatically:

Lo, I tell you a mystery. We shall not all sleep, but we shall all be changed, in a moment, in the twinkling of an eye, at the last trumpet. For the trumpet will sound, and the dead will be raised imperishable, and we shall be changed. For this perishable nature must put on the imperishable, and this mortal nature must put on immortality ... Then shall come to pass the saying that is written: 'Death is swallowed up in victory.'[9]

But what is the relationship between our earthly bodies and our changed heavenly ones? Is there any link, any connection at all? And if not, how can there be any 'recognition' of those we love in the life beyond death?

In a way, these questions have already been answered, if we accept the resurrection of Jesus as the prototype of all resurrection from death. As we have seen, there was a very real connection between the earthly body of Jesus and his risen one, but they were not identical. I have described the link as developmental, because that seemed a way of expressing the kind of unity which is involved. The second develops out of the first. It is a refinement of it, a further stage, a mutation, if we want a 'scientific' term. But it could never work the other way. The one is incomparably 'higher' and more advanced than the other. The continuity is of personality; the change involves the form in which that personality presents itself. Flesh and blood is our present form, with the limitations that that imposes. But what is to be our 'form' in the life beyond this earth?

The early Christians at Corinth put precisely that question to the apostle Paul. Here is his reply, in full.[10]

But perhaps someone will ask, 'How is the resurrection achieved? With what sort of body do the dead arrive?' Now that is talking without using your minds! In your own experience you know that a seed does not germinate without itself 'dying'. When you sow a seed you do not sow the 'body' that will eventually be produced, but bare grain, for example, or one of the other seeds. God gives the seed a 'body' according to his laws – a different 'body' to each kind of seed.

Then again, even in this world, all flesh is not identical. There is a difference in the flesh of human beings, animals, fish and birds.

There are bodies which exist in this world, and bodies which exist in the heavens. These bodies are not, as it were, in competition; the splendour of an earthly body is quite a different thing from the splendour of a heavenly body. The sun, the moon and the stars all have their own particular splendour, while among the stars themselves there are different kinds of splendour.

There are illustrations here of the raising of the dead. The body is 'sown' in corruption; it is raised beyond the reach of corruption. It is 'sown' in dishonour; it is raised in splendour. It is sown in weakness; it is raised in power. It is sown a natural body; it is raised a spiritual body. As there is a natural body so will there be a spiritual body.

It is written, moreover, that:

The first man Adam became a living soul. So the last Adam is a life-giving Spirit. But we should notice that the order is 'natural' first and then 'spiritual'. The first man came out of the earth, a material creature. The second man came from Heaven and was the Lord himself. For the life of this world men are made like the material man; but for the life that is to come they are made like the one from Heaven. So that just as we have been made like the material pattern, so we shall be made like the heavenly pattern. For I assure you, my brothers, it is utterly impossible for flesh and blood to possess the kingdom of God. The transitory could never possess the everlasting.

The dead and the living will be fitted for immortality.

Listen, and I will tell you a secret. We shall not all die, but suddenly, in the twinkling of an eye, every one of us will be changed as the trumpet sounds! The trumpet will sound and the dead shall be raised beyond the reach of corruption, and we who are still alive shall suddenly be utterly changed. For this perishable nature of ours must be wrapped in imperishability . . .

This statement repays close study, because in it Paul expresses the heart of the Christian (as compared to the pagan) doctrine of immortality. Here is no crude idea of dead bodies rising from their graves or miraculously re-assembling after cremation, but a profound picture of development from a simpler to a more complex form of life. Paul is quite clear that our earthly bodies die. They are 'perishable', with all that that implies. Those who ridicule the whole idea of resurrection must accept in fairness that Christianity has never taught that a dead human body is anything other than 'perishable'. If they wish to attack the doctrine, let them at least pay it the minimum compliment of getting it right first. Bodies die and disintegrate, and that is that, so far as the body is concerned. 'What you sow does not come to life unless it dies,' says Paul, describing what happens when a seed is planted. When the plant has fully grown, what has become of the seed itself? It has gone, disappeared – its 'life' now part of a greater, more complex being, its 'body' utterly disintegrated. And that, he argues, is what happens to our bodies at death.

He goes further. There is to be a change of *kind*. For that he uses two analogies. The first is of different kinds of 'flesh' – earthly bodies. 'Not all flesh is alike,' he argues. 'There is one kind for men, another for animals, another for birds and another for fish.'[11]

In fact, of course, he is using unscientific language. In the strictly biological sense there is very little, if any, difference between one flesh and another. Flesh, after all, is flesh. But, of course, Paul was not using the word in the biological sense. 'Flesh' in the Bible is either the lower side of human nature or – as here – simply the bodily form of an earthly creature. There is a difference between the forms of men, animals, birds, and fish, but it is a difference within limits. They have life in common, and much else: senses, appetites, animation. But within a circle of comparability they are yet distinctively different. So – he clearly implies – is life after death from life before death.

SPIRITUAL LIFE IS BETTER

His second analogy is a rather obscure one to modern eyes. 'There are celestial bodies and there are terrestrial bodies; but the glory of the celestial is one, and the glory of the terrestrial is another. There is one glory of the sun, and another glory of the moon, and another glory of the stars, for star differs from star in glory.'[12] It is tempting to read into it more than it can bear. All Paul is saying, it seems to me, is that once again within the created order there are differences within circles of comparability. Obviously the moon *is* different from the sun, and the sun is from the earth, and one star from another. But they are all bodies in space, 'heavenly bodies'. It is also very probable that, using the cosmology of his day, which saw the stars and planets in a sort of hierarchical order, he was also saying that within this limited similarity there was an ascending order of 'glory' from the lowest to the mightiest.

All of this leads on to his positive statement that spiritual (that is to say, heavenly) life is 'like' physical (that is to say, earthly) human life, but is more 'glorious'. Earthly life is perishable, crude, weak; heavenly life is imperishable, glorious, powerful. Yet there is a circle of comparability. They are not really two different things, but one is an extension or development of the other. 'But it is not the spiritual which is first but the physical, and then the spiritual.'[13] The development is not from a higher form of life to a lower one, but the opposite. There is, as we saw in the case of the risen body of Jesus, a developmental relationship between the earthly body and the resurrection body, but it is a development *upwards*. At death we move to a higher, not a lower plane of existence.

Now that is very important, if only because some 'survival' theories, including re-incarnation and many kinds of spiritualism, imply the contrary. The wispy spirits who blow trumpets and tap out pathetic messages from the beyond could never be described, surely, as 'more glorious' than living, breathing, rational, earthly human beings? 'Glory' is simply not a word one could apply to most of them or their misty world of half-reality. Equally a man re-incarnated as an animal or an insect – or even another man – could not be said to have moved upwards to a higher, more glorious mode of existence. (I realise that in most doctrines of re-incarnation there is also the opportunity to move 'upwards', but only in certain circumstances.)

So the body we are to have after death (the 'resurrection' body) is a development, a refinement of our present one, which disintegrates at death. There is a relationship between them, but the spiritual body is infinitely 'higher' and in every respect superior. The personality – the 'message' – remains, but the transmitter is a much better one.

The fact is that 'flesh and blood cannot inherit the kingdom of God'.[14] They are excellent vehicles for the message of the human personality in space and time, but quite inadequate for it in a mode of existence where space and time are meaningless concepts. That is why this great 'change' that Paul speaks of, this metamorphosis, has to take place. Just as the caterpillar has to be changed into the butterfly in order to 'inherit' the air, so we have to be changed in order to inherit 'heaven'. There is simply no alternative.

So let us stress again the most important fact involved here – that the spiritual body and the spiritual life are better, more glorious, more *real* than their physical predecessors. Once we have really got this into our thinking our whole attitude to death will be transformed. If all we have to look forward to at death is at best extinction, and at worst a shadowy ghost-existence in some twilight spirit world, then no wonder men face it with distaste and even fear. We do not enjoy the thought of ceasing to exist, but neither does a normal, life-loving human relish relegation to a kind of sub-life, which is all that most non-Christian theories of 'survival' really amount to. The best of them do, it is true, look on to some kind of blissful union with 'the ultimate', but none, it seems to me, can match the Christian emphasis on the superiority at every level and in every way of the life that begins at death. This is the great theme of the fifteenth chapter of Paul's first epistle to the Corinthians: the 'resurrection' life is a life of power, achievement, splendour, beauty. It has everything good from this earthly life, but without the things that make it earth-bound, limited and frustrating. Over everything on earth hangs the dark shadow of time. We never seem to have enough of it to do all the things we should like to do, to become the people we ought to be or to get to know others as we should like to know them. And there are other limitations: pain, failing sight and hearing, physical handicaps and so on. All of these detract from the quality and satisfaction of life on earth, though in overcoming them men have achieved nobility and greatness.

But in the life beyond death all of these are no more. 'God himself will be with them,' says John in Revelation; 'He will wipe away every tear from their eyes, and death shall be no more, neither shall there be mourning nor crying nor pain any more, for the former things have passed away.'[15] Yet in losing them, we do not lose what is essentially human. We do not become ghosts. We carry over all that is essential (the 'kernel' as Paul put it[16]), but 'God gives it a body as he has chosen.'[17]

All of which emphasises the fact that if the Christian doctrine of resurrection is true — and I have tried to show how strong and consistent it is — then there is no need for distaste or trepidation in the face of death. All that lies beyond, for those who are to be raised in Christ, is superbly good. The God who made this earth so splendid, with its wonderful variety of colour and form, its joys of human love, family, and work and its magnificence of art, music, and literature, has himself promised that the *next* life will be better. What more could any doubter ask than that?

NOTES

[1] John 20: 15.
[2] Luke 24: 30–31.
[3] John 21: 1–12.
[4] Luke 24: 38–39.
[5] Luke 24: 39–43.
[6] John 20: 19.
[7] Luke 1: 9.
[8] Romans 6: 9.
[9] 1 Corinthians 15: 51–54.
[10] 1 Corinthians 15: 35–53 (J. B. Phillips' translation).
[11] 1 Corinthians 15: 39.
[12] 1 Corinthians 15: 40–41.
[13] 1 Corinthians 15: 46.
[14] 1 Corinthians 15: 50.
[15] Revelation 21: 3–4.
[16] 1 Corinthians 15: 37.
[17] 1 Corinthians 15: 38.

Chapter Five

WHAT IS 'HEAVEN' LIKE?

It is not unreasonable of people to ask what Christians believe about heaven, but with the best will in the world it is not possible to find precise, clear, factual answers. The reasons for this are fairly obvious, of course. How could you explain to a primitive tribesman what life in a modern city is like – let alone the basic principles of television, or jet travel? Yet both of us live in the same earth environment, breathe the same air, and are subject to the same physical laws. But 'heaven', whatever it is, must be *fundamentally* different. It cannot be a space–time environment. It cannot – in any normal sense of the word – even be regarded as a 'place'. So, deprived of all those elements which enable us to describe anything in normal terms, Christians are usually reduced to saying what heaven is 'like' – a device which Jesus himself used on many occasions.

So let us begin by saying what heaven is not – a very necessary exercise, since it is caricatures of the true Christian picture of heaven which have led many to reject the whole idea as childish, pre-scientific and superstitious nonsense. These caricatures have included several produced by Christian writers, including Dr. John Robinson, the former Bishop of Woolwich, in his book *Honest to God*,[1] who argued that man 'come of age' could never be expected to accept the idea of heaven 'up in the skies'. In rejecting – rightly – the mawkish portrayals of riverside reunions 'above the bright blue sky' favoured by some Victorian hymn-writers, many people have also rejected the perfectly rational, consistent picture of heaven provided by the New Testament writers as they record the teaching of Jesus.

It simply will not do for such writers to set up these targets of straw and then solemnly (or cynically) demolish them. It is worth emphasising that Jesus never spoke of heaven in woodenly literal terms. One should also point out that apocalyptic writings like the book of Revelation were never intended to be read as scientific accounts of factual matters, and never should be. It is quite wrong to treat allegorical and metaphorical language in this unimaginative – or is it prejudiced – way?

HEAVEN IS NOT 'UP'

Heaven is not – for example – 'up'. I know that will come as a surprise to some readers, because if an idea is old enough, no matter how flimsy its basis, it is hard to eradicate it. A great deal of biblical language seems to support it as well: the very term 'ascension' – 'going up' – to describe the return of Jesus to heaven is a good example. The cosmology of the day certainly thought in terms of the earth beneath (and waters 'under the earth') with the firmament above, with heaven high above all. But in a remarkable way various biblical writers at different times put the whole idea of heaven in a totally non-material, non-space–time setting. The opening of the magnificent twenty-first chapter of Revelation is an example of this: 'I saw a new heaven and a new earth; for the first heaven and the first earth had passed away, and the sea was no more. And I saw the holy city, new Jerusalem, coming down out of heaven from God, prepared as a bride adorned for her husband; and I heard a great voice from the throne, saying, "Behold, the dwelling of God is with men" . . .'[2] There is no crude materialism here. Heaven in fact comes 'down', though actually all such spatial ideas are irrelevant to a place which is not 'in' a space–time environment. The important thing is that heaven is where God is ('the dwelling of God is with men'), and in this 'new' heaven God has drawn his people into a community in which he is going to dwell. In such a community God will wipe away every tear, and abolish pain, sorrow, and death . . . 'for the former things are passed away'.[3]

Heaven, then, is not 'up' in strictly literal terms, but 'up' is a very good word to describe something which is greatly superior to that which it replaces. Our normal usage of the word 'higher' confirms that – higher rank, higher seniority, higher skills. In none of these cases do we literally mean 'upwards', but we mean they are superior. Heaven is certainly 'up' in that sense. It is infinitely 'above' anything we know. But it is not 'up' geographically – after all, what is 'up' in Australia is 'down' in Europe. It is different, it is not material, it is greatly superior to and more glorious than anything we know on earth, but it is not 'up there', or even 'out there'. To cling to that kind of idea is to expose our faith to the peril of being discredited by materialistic science. We are not defending some dark or hidden corner of the universe where we imagine 'heaven' may be located. Heaven is not in a corner anywhere, and it will never be located by even the most powerful radio telescopes. It is simply not in their world, not in their dimension; up, down, or sideways.

Neither is heaven a matter of golden streets and harps. In the terms of their day, these simply represented the ultimate in beauty and enjoyment. Modern British people might speak of a land of endless sunshine and music, without meaning anything more than an idyllic holiday haunt. 'Heaven' is no more literally made of gold and precious stones than the promised land of Canaan literally 'flowed with milk and honey', but the image being presented is clear enough in both cases.

HEAVEN FOR EVER AND EVER?

The other prevailing fallacy about heaven concerns the whole question of duration. Many people have said to me that they would sooner be annihilated at death than spend eternity 'playing harps'. There is something decidedly unattractive to human minds about the idea of anything going on for ever and ever. 'I'd be bored stiff' people say. 'After a few thousand years you'd have done it all . . . but there'd still be endless time to come.' They make heaven sound like a wet weekend in Bradford.

In fact, as I have tried to show, time as well as space is quite irrelevant to heaven. Just as heaven has no location in space – it can't be placed on any map of the universe – so it has no location in chronology either. It is not 'in' time, and the whole idea of passing years (or any other dimension of time) in heaven is like trying to measure laughter with a ruler. It is simply not capable of that kind of description.

Heaven is where God is, we said earlier in regard to its 'place'. And heaven is *when* God is, too. God is everlasting. That is not the same thing as saying God lasts for ever. He has 'no beginning' and 'no end'. He is Yahveh (his Hebrew name), which means 'I Am' – the permanently present tense. God simply *exists*, without reference to years on a calendar. Man will be, is, and was, according to whether he is to live in the future, or live in the present, or lived in the past. God *is*. He was never younger than he is now, and he does not grow old. And that is what heaven is like. There will be no tenses there.

In passing, those who ridicule the very idea of God as eternal, without beginning or end, might care to reflect on the alternative possibilities. If there was a time when God did not exist, then he 'came into existence' and is a dependent being like we are. If there is to be a time when God ceases to exist then he is as captive to mortality as we are. By definition, 'God' is self-existent, depending on no one else and the ultimate source of being. As soon as we use the word 'God' we have to accept that it must refer to a self-existent being. Otherwise we are simply devaluing it and evacuating it of any distinctive meaning.

Having looked at some negatives about heaven, we might now try to answer the question, what is heaven like? In fact, the negatives have themselves provided some of the answers. If heaven is not located in the dimensions of space and time, then it is an entirely different mode of existence from any we have ever known or imagined. It is literally beyond comprehension. That, perhaps, is why so many modern people react negatively to heaven, or ridicule the very idea.

CLUES ABOUT HEAVEN

But the Bible does provide quite a number of helpful clues to what heaven is like. We have mentioned one — it is 'where God is, when God is'. Heaven is being with God (and hell, we might add, is being where God is not: an appalling concept).[4] So heaven is in many respects 'like' God: beauty, truth, and goodness, eternal and personal. But it is not just a series of abstract qualities. It is a mode of *living*, where relationships are important and where we can all develop a greater insight into truth and experience love as never before. 'Then I shall *know*, as I am now known,' says Paul, with deep satisfaction. 'Faith and hope will one day vanish, but love never dies.'[5]

The 'heavens' of materialistic religions (such as the *valhalla* of the Norsemen or the Elysian fields of the

Romans) are really little more than glamorised re-creations of life on earth. At the other extreme, the 'heaven' of the Eastern religions, like *nirvana*, are little more than concepts – they hardly involve 'living', in any ordinary sense of the word. But the Christian heaven avoids both extremes. It is no mere second innings of earthly existence, improved mainly by the absence of certain serious handicaps, such as pain and death; but neither is it simply a concept. In heaven we live, and live more fully and satisfyingly than ever before. And that life involves all the really important elements of what we know as life: relationships, development, knowledge, communication . . . and all in the same mode as life on earth: personality expressed through a body. The differences are enormous, but do not diminish in any way the quality of life. We shall recognise our loved ones, but by who they are rather than by what they look like. But better than that, we shall know them with a depth and insight and love as never before. Life will be transformed in the presence of its creator and sustainer.

In the light of this wonderful picture, painted for us by the biblical authors and by Jesus Christ himself, many of the most common questions about heaven can be seen in their true light, as misconceptions or irrelevancies. Will there be animals in heaven? Shall we speak English (or German, or Italian, or whatever)? What age shall we be in heaven? How can anywhere be large enough to contain all the people who have ever lived and died? And so on. The answer to them all is really the same. Because heaven cannot be distorted into our space–time terms, there are simply no words or pictures that can convey its properties to space–time minds. This may seem rather inadequate, but it is the truth. If there is a heaven at all, then almost by definition it must be beyond our comprehension.

Yet it is linked with this life. That is important. It develops from it. Human personality flowers there into its finest and most wonderful form, which is in fact the personality of Christ. This is how the apostle John put it: 'We are God's children now; it does not yet appear what we shall be, but we know that when he appears we shall be like him, for we shall see him as he is.'[6] That is man's destiny in heaven – to be 'like Christ': not Christ limited, as he was on earth, to the confines of time and flesh, but Christ risen, the great, free, timeless Christ of Easter morning. That, in a sentence, is what we shall be like in heaven; and a community of people like that is what heaven will be.

NOTES

[1] SCM Press, 1963.
[2] Revelation 21: 1–3.
[3] Revelation 21: 4.
[4] 2 Thessalonians 1: 9.
[5] 1 Corinthians 13.
[6] 1 John 3: 2.

Chapter Six

WHO GOES THERE?

There is one question which is fundamental to this whole discussion but which I have carefully avoided until now. Granted that there is a 'heaven' to which it is possible to 'go' after death, *who* goes there? Everybody? Or just some people? And if only some, on what grounds is the selection made? Obviously these questions have been raised over and over again, throughout human history. Surprisingly, almost all known religions have plumped for what is, on the face of it, the less attractive notion: that 'heaven' is by selection, and that the selection is on grounds of moral excellence.

There could be many reasons for this. The existence of a judgment after death upon the results of which would depend one's eternal destiny is a powerful incentive to obedience on earth. So 'selection' has provided religious leaders with a very powerful and effective sanction on their followers. 'Do what we say, and you will go to "heaven". Disobey, and your destiny will be destruction' . . . or whatever brand of hell the particular religion promoted.

Equally the need to attain certain moral, ethical, or heroic standards to gain entrance to heaven has spurred people on to greater effort and self-discipline. It has also, at times, spurred them to extreme generosity and filled the temple coffers of many an unscrupulous high priest.

Yet the fact remains that such a remarkable preponderance of opinion in favour of a 'selectional' system is strong *prima facie* evidence for an element of truth, or at any rate of psychological need. If an idea is persistent throughout human history, and right around the world (like the flood myths, for instance, or the idea of sacrifice in worship) then one must assume that it has some roots in reality, at one level or another. And this idea of a division in mankind at death, between those meriting 'heaven' and those deserving 'hell' is quite surprisingly persistent. There are religions which preach Universalism, of course – that all men will end up in 'heaven', whatever their behaviour on earth – but they are exceptional.

There is one very strong rational, philosophical argument for the idea of judgment after death which I find highly persuasive. It depends upon one basic premise, that there is a God and that he is good. If that idea is rejected then there is plainly no reason for believing in any kind of moral judgment after death. But if it is accepted, then the logic of the case is almost irresistible. This life is manifestly unjust. The good suffer, the unselfish are exploited, the meek are terrorised, the poor are deprived. Conversely, the evil flourish, the selfish make fortunes, the brutal oppress the meek, and the rich get richer. Tyrants die peacefully in their beds while saints expire in agony on the rack or the pyre. Of course there are plenty of exceptions. Possibly the evil are no happier in their circumstances than the good. But clearly there is no general justice. The most massive injustices go unpunished, and the most impressive unselfishness goes unrewarded.

The instinct of justice is very strong in all of us. 'It's not fair' is almost the first thing a small child learns to say. We are constantly appealing to some abstract principle of justice whose existence we assume and which we also assume is recognised by everybody else. Communists, atheists, Humanists, and believers all make this same appeal: 'It's not fair.' And yet we all also know that, in the final analysis, this life is *not* fair. With the best intentions in the world, human justice is fallible. With the worst intentions – as with a Hitler or a Stalin, for example – injustice becomes rampant.

If – as we are assuming – there is a God who is all-powerful and good, how can he possibly allow this state of affairs to continue? If he does nothing, either now or after this life, to redress such gross injustice and put down such rampant evil, he is either not all-powerful (and so cannot do it) or he is not good (and so does not care). But if he is all-powerful and good – which is what the word 'God' means to most of us – then it seems to me he *must* act to put things right. Justice on a cosmic scale must be done, and must be seen to be done, or God is not God. Very obviously he has not yet done this on earth. The strong presumption, then, is that he will do it after this life is over. And so the

Bible teaches: 'It is appointed for men to die once, and after that comes judgment.'[1] The theme of the final judgment of God, in which the mighty are put down from their thrones, the proud are scattered in the imagination of their hearts, the rich sent empty away and the hungry and poor are exalted, runs strongly through the teaching of Jesus and the apostles. It might seem that God is blind to human injustice, but one day it will be seen that he cares intensely about it, and the inequalities and evils of life on earth will be put right.

A vital part of this process is the judgment of the individual after death. Jesus described it in terms of a shepherd separating the sheep from the goats.[2] However much it may offend liberal sentiment, there can be no doubt at all that Jesus believed and taught that there was a very real possibility of people being excluded from heaven. The reason for this is quite uncomplicated. Heaven (in the Christian sense) is a community of total goodness, living in the presence of God. To allow evil into heaven would be like tossing a bad apple into a barrel of good ones: the place would no longer be totally good, and soon might become totally evil. All impurity and sin is to be excluded from heaven, simply so that it may be heaven: 'Nothing unclean shall enter it, nor any one who practises abomination or falsehood, but only those who are written in the Lamb's book of life.'[3]

WHO CAN POSSIBLY QUALIFY?

But in that case we may well ask, who can possibly hope to enter heaven? Where is the person good enough to live in a community of total goodness, without spoiling it? Surely God is going to be very lonely, sitting in the isolation of his holiness, while all his fallible, grumbling, morally imperfect creatures are excluded from this new kind of Holy Men's Club.

But the last phrase of that verse from Revelation gives the answer. It is those whose names are written in the 'Lamb's book of life' who enter heaven. Who are they? The same book tells us. They are members of a 'great multitude which no man could number, from every nation, from all tribes and peoples and tongues . . . who have washed their robes and made them white in the blood of the Lamb'.[4] The 'Lamb' is, of course, Jesus Christ, and the reference to his 'blood' is to his sacrifice of himself on the cross where he died for the forgiveness of men's sins. Through that sacrifice, Christians believe, it is possible for ordinary men and women, fallible and faulty as we all are, to be forgiven and accepted by God. In the peculiar imagery of the book of Revelation, their names are 'written' in the 'Lamb's book of life'. They will go to heaven, not on their own merits, as it were, but on his, because he has died for their sins. That is the Christian gospel. It is God's way of keeping heaven holy and yet admitting to it people no better than we are.

So the short answer to the question, who goes to heaven? is – those who have been forgiven their sins through the sacrifice of Jesus Christ. But this raises several more questions.

How, for example, can a person receive this forgiveness? The answer here is very clear and straightforward. The basic message of the New Testament is just this: turn from your sins, put your trust in Jesus Christ, and God will accept you, whoever you are.

But what about those who have never even heard of Jesus Christ? What about the countless millions who follow other religions? What about those who lived in all the long centuries before Jesus Christ was born? Rather than attempt an answer myself, I shall simply quote the apostle Paul dealing with this very question: 'When the gentiles, who have no knowledge of [God's] Law, act in accordance with it by the light of nature, they show that they have a law in themselves, for they demonstrate the effect of a law operating in their own hearts. Their own consciences endorse the existence of such a law. For there is something which condemns or commends their actions. We may be sure that all this will be taken into account in the day of true judgment, when God will judge men's secret lives by Jesus Christ, as my gospel plainly states.'[5]

WHEN SHALL WE ENTER HEAVEN?

One further question remains: when shall we enter heaven? Is it immediately at death, or at some future great 'Day of Judgment'? Whole books have been

written in the past fighting over this particular con-
troversy, with some arguing that at death we immediately pass into the presence of God, some arguing
that we 'sleep' until the day of resurrection, and others
taking all manner of considerations of, or compromises
between, these two viewpoints.

Just to make myself thoroughly unpopular with all
those who enjoy the fascinating exercise of splitting
theological hairs over these matters, I want to say that
all such argument seems to me totally irrelevant. If,
as we have seen, time is meaningless in the spiritual
world, then even to discuss intervals of time or the
passing of 'x' centuries or 'y' aeons before or after the
resurrection seem a singularly futile exercise. The
Bible itself is quite clear about this, really: a day in
God's sight is as a thousand years, and a thousand
years is as a day.[6] The 'time' taken for the metamorphosis between the physical and the spiritual world is
given by Paul as 'the twinkling of an eye'.[7] When
Christ returns to earth, as the Bible teaches he will, to
inaugurate the final judgment of mankind, those who
are alive at the time will 'not precede those who have
fallen asleep'.[8] All will be raised together, in one in-
stant of time and with no conscious elapsing of time
between their individual moments of death and the
moment of resurrection. And at that moment we shall
enter heaven.

Yet, in fact, 'enter' is the wrong word. As we have
seen, heaven is not a place, in the geographical sense,
but a mode of existence, and it is 'entered' not by any
physical journey – the 'soul' winging its way through

the void of space to some distant celestial destination – but by a spiritual one. In a very real sense we can make that journey now. As Paterson Smyth wrote, 'Though there is a special place which shall be Heaven, yet, if Heaven means a state of mind rather than a place of residence, though it is a place of residence too, if Heaven means to be something rather than to go somewhere, though it means to go somewhere too, then the answer is easy. We enter heaven by a spiritual, not by a natural act. We begin Heaven here on earth . . . by taking a journey from a bad state of mind to a good state of mind – from that state of mind which is enmity against God to that of humble, loyal, and loving obedience to Christ. It is not so much that we have to go to Heaven. We have to do that too. But Heaven has to come to us first. Heaven has to begin in ourselves.'[9]

READY FOR DEATH

And it can begin now. 'Eternal life' is something that can invade physical life, seeping back into the life lived on earth from the life to be lived in heaven. That is how the great saints and mystics have lived, with eternity already in their hearts. And that is the best possible preparation for the moment of death, whenever it is to come to us. Those who have begun a 'life in Christ' on earth find the transition between the two worlds so easy as to be almost imperceptible. Many witnesses confirm this – of the joy and even eagerness with which those who have lived close to

God on earth face the prospect of entering into an even closer relationship with him in heaven. As Paul puts it, 'For me to live is Christ, and to die is gain.'[10] If life means being with Christ, then death must be gain because it will mean a closer relationship with him, with all the barriers of mortality and sin broken down.

Leslie Weatherhead puts into words the experience of many priests, ministers, and doctors who have watched people die. 'I have seen a number of people die,' he writes, 'and I have made enquiries of nurses and doctors. You'll appreciate that most people die following a state of unconsciousness. Either they are in a coma or are drugged. But I have sat at the bedside of a man who was dying and conscious to the end. He gripped my hand and I must have gripped his more tightly than I thought I was doing, for he said, "Don't hold me back. I can see through the gates. It's marvellous."

'If you have seen, as I have, a woman so ill that she couldn't lift her head from the pillow, if you had seen her sit up, her eyes open with tremendous delight, and joy in her face, if you had heard her call the name of a beloved husband who had been dead twenty years, you would find it strangely convincing. People may say it was probably an hallucination, or a trick of the brain. All I can say is that it was very convincing to the onlooker that she really was in touch with the beloved dead and that he was coming back to welcome her.'[11] Dr. Weatherhead claimed to have collected dozens of similar instances. Indeed, he goes so far as to claim, on the basis of his enquiries made over a long period of time, that 'never once has anybody died in mental unhappiness'. Death is 'an extremely happy experience'. He even quotes a physician to the royal family who said when he was dying, 'If I had the strength to hold a pen I would tell mankind what a wonderful thing it is to die.'

If this is true for people in general, then surely for those who can look to meeting a God they have loved for many years but never seen, death will be a great joy. It is all a question of perspective. We may well fear the idea of dying. Most of us do. But for those whose trust is in Christ there cannot be fear at the thought of death. The only people who rationally may fear death are those who know that God exists, and yet have lived their lives as though he did not.

We began this book by looking at the way modern man regards death: fascinated by it, yet repelled, because it strikes at the roots of his self-sufficiency. We end it by affirming that for modern man, as for all men everywhere and in every age, death is not the end. It is not the end of life, or love, or beauty. It is not the end of anything good, worth while, or lovely. It is not the end of those we love, nor is it the end of our own spiritual and moral development. Like sailors looking out over the water, we can only see as far as the horizon that men call death. But beyond that horizon lies more, so much more; hidden from our eyes, but revealed, item by item, to our minds and our hearts by faith, and through the words of Jesus. Death is not the final enemy of man. That is evil. Death is the final enemy of man's final enemy. Beyond it lies a new kind of life, where evil has no place at all.

NOTES

[1] Hebrews 9: 27.
[2] Matthew 25: 31–46.
[3] Revelation 21: 27.
[4] Revelation 6: 9, 14.
[5] Romans 2: 14–16 (J. B. Phillips' translation).
[6] 2 Peter 3: 8.
[7] 1 Corinthians 15: 52.
[8] 1 Thessalonians 4: 15.
[9] *The Gospel of the Hereafter*, Hodder.
[10] Philippians 1: 21.
[11] *Life Begins at Death*, Denholm House Press.

Bibliography

Anderson, J. N. D., *The Evidence for the Resurrection*, IVP

Lewis, C. S., *A Grief Observed*, Faber

Stephens, Simon, *Death Comes Home*, Mowbray's

Toynbee, Arnold (and others), *Man's Concern with Death*, Hodder and Stoughton

Vianney, Gina, *Martin*, Redemptorist Press

Weatherhead, Leslie, *Life Begins at Death*, Denholm Press

Winslow, Jack, *The Gate of Life*, Hodder and Stoughton

THE CHRISTIAN BOOK PROMOTION TRUST

This book is published in association with the Christian Book Promotion Trust, 32, Dover Street, London W1A 2AP, a small non-denominational registered charity whose aims are to assist the advancement of the Christian Religion.